COLLATERAL HOPE

COLLATERAL HOPE

A Personal Journey from Darkness to Faith

DENA PETTY

Petty Four Publishing

ISBN: 979-8-9934853-0-0 paperback
LCCN: 2025920705
Cover design: The Killion Group, Inc.
Formatting: Dallas Hodge, dalhodge56@gmail.com
Editing: Cher Stein, cher@thewriteperspective.net
   Publisher: Petty Four Publishing
   Website: https://www.denapetty.com/

To my family,
God blessed me with the knowledge
I am loved just for who I am
through the love I feel from
each and every one of you.
And to my husband Todd,
thank you for calling me beautiful
almost every day of our marriage.
I thank God every day for doing life with you!

TABLE OF CONTENTS

INTRODUCTION

Looking from the outside, it's understandable that people might have a hard time believing the stories of my life. What the world sees is a passionate founder and leader of a growing non-profit: a woman married to her handsome, talented best friend for nearly forty years. They see a devoted mother of an athletically gifted son who was drafted into the NFL and a selfless daughter saving lives every day as an ICU nurse.

The perfect family. The perfect life.

At first glance, it seems idyllic. However, things are rarely as they appear. The pieces you see never tell the whole story.

Few people know the harsh reality of my youth or the journey that brought me to where I am today. They don't know the darkness of my past, shaped by two people who should have loved, nurtured, and protected me—my parents—who instead chose abuse and abandonment.

Despite appearances, I shouldn't be here, something you'll come to understand as you read on. But I am here for a purpose, and I believe the same is true for you. We each have a unique calling on our lives.

Writing this book did not come easily, but my motivation has always been to encourage others to embrace their own callings—no matter what they've been through, where they find themselves today, or the choices they regret. It would be easy to remain wounded, stifled, frozen in fear or defeat. However, choosing joy, hope, compassion, and purpose is a powerful decision not only for ourselves but for those who look to us for light.

We can let go of shame and guilt. Hope, healing, and meaning are possible. In the words of St. Francis of Assisi, "All the darkness in the world cannot extinguish the light of a single candle."

As we prepare to take this journey together, I want you to know that, like many who've endured trauma, there are gaps in my memory. Some describe it as dissociation: a subconscious act of self-preservation that shields the mind from pain.

What I share in the pages ahead is based on my best recollections, stories and revelations as I experienced them.

Many childhood moments feel fuzzy or are missing altogether. When I'm with the few family members I still keep in touch with, it can be awkward when they say, "Remember when…?" I usually just smile and shrug. Others may recall things differently, but this is my truth.

SECTION ONE:

Surrounded by Darkness

CHAPTER ONE:
REVEALING THOUGHTS

Don't look at him.
Don't move.
Stay still and very quiet.
He will calm down and not notice me.

These thoughts were ever present when it came to life with my father. My earliest memories are of making myself as small as possible to avoid his wrath.

It's not that there weren't moments of calm or affection, but there was always a lingering sense that things could shift into rage without warning. There was a lifetime of evidence to back the threat of menace.

Why is she so cruel?
Why does she hate me?

While these might sound like the sentiments of any angsty teenager, they encapsulated my entire relationship with my mother from toddlerhood until I severed all ties at age eighteen.

There were varying degrees of cruelty and manipulation. When combined with the withholding of love that turned to jealousy and contempt, it was nearly enough to break me. Saying that out loud brings a pain of its own. I built what I thought was impenetrable armor, but I was wrong. Nearly dead wrong. (More on that later.)

Rationalization without Excuses

Before I share the specific experiences I endured, it's important to acknowledge the generational trauma woven into both of my parents' bloodlines. I don't share this to excuse or justify their behaviors or choices, but simply to recognize the lasting impact of unhealed generational trauma.

My life is a flicker of light in a chasm of darkness. It would be easy to remain wounded, stifled, frozen in fear and defeat. Choosing joy, hope, compassion, and purpose is a daily decision.

It's something I practice with daily intention. I work on it by asking myself: *Why did I think that? Why did I say that? Why did I do that?*

When I ask, "Why did I think that?" I begin to examine my inner thoughts more closely. Often, what seems normal inside my mind sounds very different when I pause to reflect or speak it aloud with someone I trust. Many times, my thoughts turn out to be irrational, incomplete, or even fictional. This process has shown me how easily my mind can drift away from truth. Or worse, spiral into a relentless cycle.

That cycle felt like a merry-go-round I couldn't get off. My thoughts circled endlessly, sometimes tormenting me to the point that I felt powerless to stop them. One painful season stands out. I had been deeply hurt, and the wound stirred up old memories I thought were long buried. The situation replayed in my mind again and again, as though stuck on repeat. No matter how much I prayed or tried to push it away, I found myself returning to the same reel of pain.

In time, God would begin to interrupt these endless cycles with glimpses of His truth. But at that point, I was still caught in the loop, desperate for a way forward.

Mother: The Withholding Wound

I always found it amazing that my mother, growing up in a humble farmhouse in east Texas—a literal working farm—turned out so self-absorbed and critical, but she was. What shocked me even more was how blind she was to her own faults. She was quick to point out the flaws of others, especially mine, but never own. She constantly mentioned how she "held water" and needed her water pills. That wasn't water she was holding.

Her words had a bite to them. She smiled easily, but her words carried a rudeness that lingered. Her smile felt like an inside joke I could never understand. She seemed to relish the pain her comments caused.

I cringed at compliments because they were always followed by a bite that wasn't worth it:

"Your clothes are too big from losing weight… but don't worry, you'll put it back on."

Little did either of us know her sharp and biting words would become one of my greatest inspirations. For every cruelty, denial, and outburst, something rose up in me. Deep down, I knew I didn't deserve it.

With each act of cruelty, I grew stronger. What was meant to destroy me instead forged me into a woman destined to love, forgive, grow, and overcome as God intended. But when I was a little girl, it brought confusion—and pain.

My mother made a lot of mistakes growing up, as we all do. But she never learned from them and always left a trail of hurt and disappointment behind her. If she just could have learned from her mistakes or even say the words, "I'm sorry." Her life might have turned out differently. And I might have been a less wounded daughter.

She left the childhood farm to pursue opportunities in the city. Whether she was chasing a better life or escaping a difficult one remains unclear.

My mother had a fondness for parties and for being in relationships with many men. At sixteen, she experienced an unintended pregnancy and opted for an abortion—something rare and stigmatized in the 1950s.

That decision deeply affected her. Unfortunately, it didn't change her patterns. Instead, it led to more chaos, more poor choices, and the continued cycle of generational trauma.

To understand her choices, you have to go back a generation.

My mother's mother, Granny, was born in 1896 to wealthy plantation owners in Louisiana. She was considered a beauty in her youth. In the 1920s, she met and married my grandfather, and they moved to Texas to start a new life. Granny's past followed her.

Granny had been molested in childhood by an uncle. A violation buried in family silence. That same uncle tracked her down years later. My grandfather, fiercely protective, took a shotgun and shot the man's arm off. The uncle lived, but was forever marked by the weight of what he had done.

Years later, when the uncle died as an old man, people cried and mourned him. At his funeral, an elderly woman leaned over the casket, kissed him, and whispered, "He was such a good man." Another woman nearby replied, "If he was such a good man, why is he missing an arm?"

The truth always finds its way into the shadows.

Family stories, even the hidden ones, can be healing. Understanding our family's struggles helps break cycles. It allows us to stop shame and guilt from traveling any further. The truth is hard to face. But eventually, it rises.

Looking back, I believe shame played a powerful role in the choices my mother made. I don't know what she truly believed about herself, but I wonder if, like Adam, she, too, was hiding.

> But the Lord God called to the man, "Where are you?"
> He answered, "I heard you in the garden, and I was afraid because I was naked; so I hid." (Genesis 3:9–10 NIV)

Shame makes us hide. Not just from God, but from ourselves. From healing. From truth. I believe my mother spent much of her life running from the very places God wanted to meet her.

After the abortion, she met a man she claimed to love. She brought him home to meet the family, but my grandfather—hardworking, protective, and sharp—saw through him immediately. I don't know exactly what happened, but my grandfather kicked him out of the house.

My mother and this man left the farmhouse and returned to the city, but not before stealing all of Granny and Grandpa's silver coins. Granny had collected them before the Great Depression.

Grandpa was right. The man wasn't good.

Back in the city, she got pregnant again. He left. Not surprisingly.

She gave the baby up for adoption. From what I've heard, he had a wonderful family and a good life. For that, I'm grateful.

After a string of traumatic relationships, still unhealed and still repeating history, my mother met my father. She met him one night, and that same night, she left with him. She never returned to her parents' home again.

They married and tried to live the American dream: three kids, a dog, a home in the suburbs. They signed us up for sports. Took us fishing. Put us in private school.

Sounds amazing, doesn't it?

I'm sure we looked normal to people on the outside. But the reality was, a marriage built on sand, not rock. It was shaky from the start.

Two broken people came together without doing the work to heal or even discover who they were as children of God.

They were created for purpose. So were we, the children they brought into that unstable home. We were meant to be loved. Meant to be blessings. Meant to receive unconditional love.

That never happened.

I don't know why I feared my mother so much. She wasn't quick with her tongue or physically abusive, at least, not at first.

I think it was the cruelty in her words. The looks of disgust she gave me. The soft place a mother is supposed to offer. On of nurturing and consoling. I never knew that.

She withheld affection. She never said "I love you." She didn't hug me. That kind of withholding became its own cruelty.

When I was a little girl, she had a hold on me. She manipulated me and created a fear that wasn't rational.

One night, I had a terrifying dream that woke me up screaming. I was about four or five. My parents couldn't calm me down, so they brought me to the emergency room. I don't remember all the details, but I know the dream was about being lost and unable to find my mother.

I told the doctor I had a stomachache. That wasn't true. I just didn't know how to explain the fear. Looking back, I believe it was my subconscious working through the fear and rejection I felt during the day.

I was emotionally abandoned by my mother. And even as a little girl, I knew that wasn't how it was supposed to be.

Our minds are incredible. They know how to protect us when pain is too deep to process.

Much of my childhood is a blur, whole seasons I can't recall. When relatives reminisce, I usually just smile and nod, with no flicker of personal remembrance.

I'm not a psychologist, and I won't pretend to understand how memory works. All I know is that God knows them all. He has protected me in ways I can't explain. And in His perfect plan, some memories are vivid… and some are mercifully out of reach.

One clear memory that has stayed with me over the years is from when I was about seven.

We moved often during my childhood. Based on my recollection, I attended thirteen different schools.

Starting over at a new school became normal for me. I hated those first days. Trying to make friends, hoping someone would talk to me before recess.

Because if no one did, recess could feel like a lifetime. Standing alone on the school yard, day after day, made me an easy target for bullying.

On one brisk, cool morning in the Deep South, my mom took me to register at my newest school. The next day was my first day. I have one bright memory tied to that moment. Aunt Nell.

She was nothing like my mother. Aunt Nell was my light, always shining small glimmers of hope into the darkness of my childhood.

On this occasion, she made me feel special by sewing me a school outfit. She was incredibly talented, a gifted seamstress. She seemed to be able to do anything.

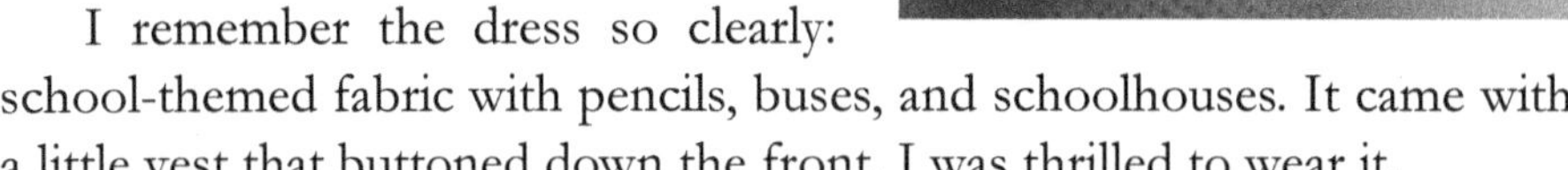

I remember the dress so clearly: school-themed fabric with pencils, buses, and schoolhouses. It came with a little vest that buttoned down the front. I was thrilled to wear it.

My mom gave me ten cents for milk and sent me on my way.

I left the house in my new dress, walking through dewy grass under a blue sky. I remember thinking: *My shoes are going to be wet all day. Yuck.*

But I didn't mind walking. I always looked for interesting bugs or found rocks to kick as I went. The cool fall air felt fresh, and the world was quiet. No cars passed. No neighbors were outside.

I was seven and I didn't think much about where I was going. Until I realized I had no idea where I was. I didn't know the route. I didn't know the name of the school. I didn't know my new address. I didn't know our phone number.

I was completely lost.
So I just kept walking.

Eventually, I found the school. I don't know how. I was too young to track time, but

I remember the panic.
The way fear closed in.

That constant feeling of being unsafe, unseen, unprotected—like a bear was breathing down my neck—was normal for me.

That moment was the start of my training in how not to panic, even when fear was roaring in my mind.

Not because I wasn't scared, but because I learned panic never helped.

Keep moving.
No one's coming to save me.

What I realize now is how cruel that was. Even at the time, I remember wondering: *Did she do this on purpose?*

If she did, *why?*

What did I do wrong?

But the worst part wasn't the confusion. It was the realization: She didn't just dislike me.

She didn't love me.

Father: The Transactional Wound

People attract what they carry inside.

My mother left with him the night they met and never looked back. That's how it began. It wasn't a fairytale romance. It was two wounded people deciding they were good enough for one another.

My father, unfortunately, was a deeply broken soul. He didn't like anyone, but he loved himself immensely.

Which is to say, he couldn't love anyone else.

He was full of unresolved trauma, and over time, he developed a warped view of himself. A kind of personal psychosis. In his mind, he was above everyone. Everyone else was a sucker. A loser.

Especially women.

He believed women existed to be dominated, controlled, and used for his benefit. Everyone he met was a transaction. An opportunity to take.

He talked about money constantly. Later, I realized money wasn't just important to him—it was his god. And people, including me, were just tools to help him get more of it.

He traveled to Mexico often. He ran an import business, selling Mexican arts and crafts. Eventually, he bought a small building downtown and set up shop. After being robbed at gunpoint more than once, he decided it was time to move on.

But he still had inventory to sell, so he looked to me.

I remember him saying something like, "She's so cute. How could anyone say no to her?"

He filled up my little red wagon and sent me door to door, selling pottery and glass-blown swans. I must not have been that cute. I remember a lot of "no's."

I didn't understand it then, but I wasn't the only one shaped by poverty and rejection.

My father grew up on the streets of Oklahoma City. He was a Native American boy who knew nothing but poverty and discrimination.

He was one of eight brothers. No sisters. Their father came around only occasionally. Just long enough to conceive another child.

Later, I learned their father was abusive. Extremely violent. He beat all the boys. I was told once he hit my dad across the back with a 2x4. That was his version of discipline.

I didn't know whether to feel sorry for him or afraid of what that pain had turned him into.

He also had women all over the city, with children no one could count. To my knowledge, my dad only spoke to him once in my entire childhood.

I remember the day.

The rotary phone rang in the kitchen. My mother answered and said, "Del, it's your father." My dad got up, put the phone to his ear, and didn't say a word.

He hung up.

His father died shortly after that.

That was that.

Dad used to tell stories about going without food. About seeing his breath in the air during Oklahoma winters because they had no heat.

I remember staring at his feet as a little girl. His toes were mangled. Bent and crooked from wearing shoes that didn't fit as a child. None of the boys had shoes until they started school at six, and even then, they wore them until they fell apart.

They bought everything for themselves. They hustled. Washed dishes. Boxed when they were old enough.

My father was respected by his brothers. They admired his toughness. Admired that he could knock someone out with one punch. His hands were massive. Knuckles thick and broken from fights. They talked about him fondly. Bragged about how people feared him.

Even with my limited understanding as a kid, I didn't see anything to admire. Where the adults saw someone to copy, I saw meanness to avoid at all costs.

He looked angry all the time. I learned early on it was best to stay out of his way.

I remember Grandma Evans, my father's mother, as a strong, Native-looking woman with jet-black hair and piercing dark eyes. She was mean. And ruled the roost. Even though her sons were tough street kids—my dad known as the toughest—she had the upper hand. Always.

One rare visit sticks with me.

The house was loud. All the brothers and their wives were talking over each other. The cousins were running and playing. The TV blared a football game of course.

I never understood why it had to be so loud.

The men were watching, yelling, commentating. The women talked. The kids filled the room with noise.

Then Grandma Evans walked in.

She shuffled right up to the TV, changed the channel from football to WWE wrestling, and sat down. She didn't wait until the game was over. She didn't ask permission.

> She just did it.
> And nobody said a word.
> Not even my father.
> They just shook their heads and moved on.
> I was shocked.
> Mesmerized.

As a little girl, I didn't know what to make of it. The same man who ruled our house with silence and anger bowed to her without a word. It made no sense to me.

> In our house, it was different.

My mother, though cold, calculating, and emotionally distant, was still dominated by my father. What he said went. Period. The unwritten rule: keep Dad happy. Don't rock the boat.

It was obvious he hated women. He thought they were stupid. He voiced his distain openly about women relatives, drivers, actresses on TV. Even my mom.

But somehow, his mother had all the power. How is it that Grandma Evans had so much power? When all others, including my mother, had none? He feared his mother. I didn't understand it. It deeply confused my young mind.

I was told that Grandma Evans hated all white people. I guess that's why she didn't like me. I was half white.

As the family tells, it her hatred came from a wound passed down through generations. Somewhere in our ancestry, two family members, one Chickasaw, one Choctaw, signed the Trail of Tears roster.[1]

One of them received the allotted 160 acres through the Dawes Act. The land was supposed to help Native families establish farms and futures.[2]

But over time, that land was taken. Controlled by non-Natives.

> Gone.

The trauma of that loss ran deep. When her father died, she was supposed to inherit land but there was nothing left. What should have been security became destitution. Hope soured into bitterness.

That bitterness didn't just stay with her. It seeped into how she raised her sons. Into how they saw the world. And how they survived.

Poverty is cruel.

People who grow up in poverty fight to look normal. But the basics—things most people take for granted—feel out of reach.

Clean clothes. Clean homes. Clean bodies.
It all takes money and time.

Hot water isn't free. Laundry detergent isn't free. And if you don't have a washing machine, you need quarters and hours you might not have. You don't just toss a load in and relax.

You plan.
You hustle.
You make do.
And you wait.

My dad and his brothers were dirty as kids, not because they wanted to be, but because they were poor. Clean was a privilege, not a given.

In the 1950s, being a "greaser" was cool. Slicked-back hair, pomade, *that* look. For my dad, it was more than a style. It was a way to **look** clean without **being** clean.

I remember him telling a story about learning what cleanliness really meant. He didn't always live it out in later years but something in him had shifted. At least a little.

My father eventually landed a job with IBM as a systems analyst. He created punch cards for early computer programs—the foundation of modern software.

It was a big deal. A real job.
A professional role.

He told me that in the 1960s, when he got hired, he was required to wear a suit and tie every day. He only had one suit. One tie. He wore them every single day.

Until one day, a coworker quietly pulled him aside and said, "You smell. You need to clean your clothes."

Surprisingly, my dad appreciated that moment. He told me no one had ever said anything like that to him before. He realized how hard it must have been for that man to tell him the truth.

It baffled me.

This was a man who thought everyone else was stupid.

Beneath him.
But he respected that honesty.

He was Native American. Brilliant. Extremely poor.

But he was determined.

He earned a journalism scholarship to the University of Oklahoma. He got to attend every game and report from the sidelines for the school newspaper.

When he talked about college though, it wasn't with pride. It was mostly complaints.

He said most students were "suckers." Wasting time in class instead of just taking the book home, learning it, and passing the test.

"You learn how to learn fast," he'd say. "You can't waste time when you only have so many hours to work and go to school. You gotta eat."

He never finished. He dropped out.

I don't know all the details, but I'm not surprised. My father rarely finished anything. If it got hard, he quit. And he always had a reason—someone else to blame. Or just the same old excuse: "I had to eat."

One of my earliest memories is waking up in the middle of the night to shouting.

I sat up in bed, startled. *What was that?*

I got out of bed and peeked around the corner from the living room into the kitchen. My parents were screaming at each other.

I was scared. Confused.

I didn't know why they were yelling, but I knew it was bad. My mom stood at the kitchen sink. My dad was in her face, shouting. She was leaning back, trapped. But I remember something strange on her face: a smile. Or maybe a smirk. I recognize that smile now.

I remember feeling lost in those moments, like I couldn't fully understand what people were saying.

TV shows didn't make sense. Conversations didn't make sense.

I would think, *One day I'll understand… but why can't I now?*

I listened. But I didn't understand.

Then there was the blood.

My father was on crutches, wearing a cast. His clothes were soaked in blood. That image was frightful. He was yelling. Angry. Again.

I heard pieces of the story: a car accident. The car was totaled. Hit by a train.

He said he went door to door, begging for help. Several houses. Losing a lot of blood. Finally, someone answered.

I didn't know why he was covered in blood. I didn't know why he was so angry at my mother. But I remember thinking: *Something is very wrong.*

Anger was normal in our home and it never made sense. It never matched the situation. Minor problems turned into explosions. Everything was unfair. Everyone was stupid. The smallest spark always became an inferno.

But this night was different. This wasn't just anger. This was something else.

Later, I found out the truth.

He had been cheating on my mom. He was with another woman. They were parked on the railroad tracks when a train hit them. They didn't hear the horn. Didn't see the light.

The car was shoved down the tracks. His leg went through the floorboard and was dragged under the car until it stopped. I don't know what happened to the woman. I pray she survived.

In true form, my dad blamed the train company. He sued them for not having a light on the train, for not using a horn.

But would he have seen it? Would he have heard it? Would he have had time to move the car? Probably not.

He won the lawsuit. Used the money to buy a catfish farm in Holden, Louisiana. That was just like him though. Connected to politicians, always knowing someone, always blaming someone else.

That night changed me.

Watching my parents fight. Hearing what I could understand. Seeing him covered in blood. It was earth-shattering.

I thought we were just another family. Again, the realization, we were not normal. Not even close.

Still, even in the chaos, there were moments of wonder. Pieces of light, and I held them with the fierceness of the desperate.

CHAPTER TWO:
THE STRUGGLE FOR SELF-WORTH

The Scent of Rescue

Some memories are sharp.
Others are soft.
The soft ones confused me the most.

Other kids had parents who spent time with them—family trips, meaningful conversations, shared meals that felt warm.

We didn't have that. At first, though, we looked the part.

In my early elementary years, Mom cooked dinner every night. She asked about our day at school. My brother and I played outside with the neighborhood kids like everything was normal.

We even had a dog, Bebe. I loved that dog. We all did.

Bebe had a litter of puppies once, and I couldn't get enough of them. I'd lie in the grass while they climbed over me, licking my face, nipping at my toes and fingers. I'd laugh, squeal, and fall over as they chased me around the yard. I remember looking up and seeing my mom laughing, too. A real, joyful smile.

That moment sticks with me.
It was beautiful.
It was real.

My father was cruel to most people, and to most animals. But he loved Bebe. When Bebe died, he cried. Hard.

It surprised me. His grief was so intense. This man, who was usually cold and sharp, fell apart over a dog.

It confused me.

Just like the time he bent down, looked me in the face, and said,

"She sure is going to be a beauty when she grows up."

I was standing between him and my mom when he said it.

She snapped. "Don't tell her that!"

And just like that, the moment disappeared. I dropped my head and walked out of the room, shame rising in my chest. Why was it wrong to say? I hadn't asked for the compliment. But somehow, I felt like I'd done something bad. Stolen something from her.

Maybe she felt like he wasn't talking to their daughter, but to another woman. That moment was the rarest thing: my father being gentle. Then, like a puff of smoke taken on a breeze, it was gone.

I was grateful for that tiny glimpse of something soft. But I also learned how quickly kindness could become a threat.

Light, hope, and laughter came in flickers. Like candlelight in the dark. When things grew heavy or unpredictable, I held on to the good memories.

My love for nature, the sea, and its creatures came from weekends spent on the water. To me, it was the ocean.

We lived in New Orleans, and nearly every weekend, we'd head south toward the Gulf, the wetlands, and the endless horizon that, in my child's eyes, could only be called "the ocean."

And my God, how I loved it.

My dad had a Chris-Craft boat. To me, it was the most beautiful thing I'd ever seen—white with marine blue trim, as big as a house. I didn't notice the chipping paint or the patched planks. I just saw a boat that promised adventure.

Below deck were small bunks and the faint smell of saltwater and diesel. Trawler nets sat curled in the stern. Rods lined the rails. That boat was always ready to launch—into water, into wonder.

We'd leave before dawn. Mom packed food and water, and I'd wake up with excitement about what might be in the nets or at the end of a line. Sometimes we trawled in open water. Sometimes we stayed in the shallows.

We always ended the day at the oyster bar—not a restaurant, but a real oyster reef, a mound of shells where we could grab fresh oysters right from the Gulf. We'd toss them on the deck, grit and all. Trawling moved too slow for a young girl. But the water never did.

I'd dangle my hand beside the boat, watching the waves part, wondering how birds flew so long without flapping their wings. The sun would sparkle across the surface, and once in a while, a dolphin would breach, mist spraying from its blowhole.

It was magic.

That's where my lifelong fascination with science, nature, and God's creation was born. On that old, broken boat. I loved every second of it.

Sometimes we'd anchor near a deserted island. My parents fished while I explored. With fascination I turned over seashells, followed crabs, laughed at hermit crabs fighting over one shell when there were dozens nearby.

They were feisty.
They reminded me of people.

The murky Gulf waters were alive with stingrays, crabs, flounder, redfish, speckled trout, oysters, drum fish, and grouper. I learned the difference between what my dad called "good fish" and "trash fish." He hated the trash fish. If he caught one, he'd throw it on the bank to die.

I hated that.
Why did they have to die?
What made them trash?

Once, he flung a stingray onto the shore. I ran to it and saw it gasping. I couldn't stand it.

Then something moved.
I screamed.
Mom came running.

She knelt down and said, "Let's put her back. She's having babies."
We used driftwood to gently roll her into the water, careful of her barbed tail. Stingrays can be dangerous, but she didn't look dangerous to me. She looked perfect.
The babies kept coming. Tiny, perfect copies, swimming around her still body.

I cried.
I was happy for them.
But sad for her.
Why did she have to die?
Why was she called trash?
Was it because she could protect herself?

Then her wings twitched. Her body stirred. And just like that, she swam away, her babies trailing behind.

Even now, the smell of diesel brings it all back.

That scent—the thick black smoke of a tugboat or a slow leak in the hull— pulls me back in time. Like a mental rip current, that smell can capture my thoughts. Back then, before GPS and weather apps, my reckless father would head straight into the open Gulf. Maybe it didn't seem like a big deal to others who knew the strength of the water. But for someone who grew up landlocked in Oklahoma City, Dad had no respect for the water's power. Old boats take on water. Storms roll in fast.

As an adult, I still can't believe how dangerous it was—him taking his family out like that. And yet we went.

Almost every time, it seemed, the boat would break down. Out in the middle of nowhere. No land in sight. No boats. No wind.

He'd throw things. Swear. Rage.
And I would disappear.
I learned early: Don't look at him.
Don't move.
Stay very still.
He'll calm down.
Maybe he won't notice me.

One day, the boat died again. We drifted in the eerie stillness. So we fished. Three hooks on every line. Three fish each time. Everyone was laughing. Until the wind picked up.

The sky dimmed. The water chopped. Rain started slow, then fast. Waves threw us side to side. Mom turned on the light bulb near the helm, trying to make it feel safe.

But then she grabbed the wrong thing, grasped the light itself to steady herself.

Her body convulsed. She was being electrocuted. Dad lunged and knocked her to the floor.

She lived. We all did. But we were still in the middle of the storm.

Eventually, the sky cleared. A tugboat appeared, belching black smoke and trailing that thick, familiar smell.

Diesel.
The scent of a rescue.

We flagged it down. Tossed a rope. And like so many times before, they pulled us home.

That smell.
Awful.
Unforgettable.

It meant one thing to me.

We were rescued.
Again.

Not a Protector

Fishing was a big part of my childhood. But not every memory on the water was magical. Some were terrifying because even in the places I loved, I was never truly safe.

Every time we went out on the water, it felt like an adventure. Unpredictable and exciting. Maybe that's why I still love it.

I have beautiful memories: sunlight dancing on the surface, nature humming in its rhythm, the comfort of the sun looking different depending on where we were.

So when my dad said, "Come with me to the coast," I was ready.

Another adventure.

It felt a little strange that it was just the two of us, but I didn't question it.

There was no boat in tow. Instead, he had a new toy, something he was proud of. A seining net.

A long net, about four feet tall and forty feet long, with 2x4s fastened to each end. He explained it was used to catch fish by surrounding them in the water.

"How fun," I thought.

Instead of a beach or boat launch, we drove to a fishing wharf, an old, run-down place with rotting docks and rusted boats tied to pilings.

Narrow waterways fed the area. The ocean wasn't in sight. The water was dark and still. The shoreline was littered with half-submerged scrap metal, like ruins from a forgotten industry.

No people.
No noise.
Just us.

"Perfect," my dad said, unloading the net.

He barked instructions:

"Walk straight into the water. Hold the 2x4 upright so the fish can't escape. I'll unroll the net behind you. Don't stop. I'll tell you when to turn."

I hesitated.

Wait. *I'm* the one pulling the net into the water?

But I didn't dare say anything.
His anger was too close.
I knew better than to question him.

So I did what he said. The yelling started immediately.

"Hold it straight! Keep walking!"
The water rose higher.
Up to my chest.
Then to my chin.

Every now and then, I'd step into a hole and drop suddenly, gasping for air as the net tilted and pulled.

"You're letting the fish out!" he yelled.
I was struggling.
Something hit the net.
Hard.
It thrashed.
Knocked me sideways.

My dad didn't ask if I was okay. He just screamed:
"Hold it straight! You're letting the fish out!"
I didn't panic. I got my footing, walked slowly back to the shoreline, still listening to his orders.
Coughing up water, I joined him to haul in the net. We pulled it in, waiting for the final section to reveal our catch.

The middle was shredded.
A huge hole.

To my young eyes, it looked enormous.

No fish.
No celebration.
No apology.
Just cussing.

No recognition of what he had asked me to do. He muttered and jerked the gear around.
"Help me roll this up," he snapped.
Back into the car. No words about what just happened.
I thought about that day for years. What was it that hit the net? Much later, I spoke to a helicopter pilot who flew crews out to oil rigs off the Louisiana coast. He told me that area was full of sharks. Bull sharks, especially. From the air, you can see them circling the shallows.
I believe that's what hit the net. A bull shark.
And I believe the only reason I'm here to tell this story is because my heavenly Father protected me. Even when my earthly father did not.
A house, not a home.

Feeling safe.
Loved.
Nurtured.

It was something I longed for, but I couldn't have told you that then. I didn't know how to name it. I just knew something was wrong.

I wanted my mother to love me and care for me. I wanted my father to protect me, to make me feel safe.

Even as a little girl, I determined: *That wasn't going to be my life.* I was on my own.

Keeping the bear out of the room meant staying silent.

Not crying.
Not asking for anything.

There was a time when I was little, my Mom cooked most nights and asked about school. It wasn't warm, exactly, but there was a routine that gave life a kind of structure. Looking back, I think she was trying in her own way.

But as I got older, that rhythm faded. The meals got simpler. The house grew darker. And the distance between us widened.

What once felt like effort gave way to resignation. Eventually, even Hamburger Helper was too much to ask for without resentment. There were always mysteries surrounding my father.

We were poor, but he had money. He was Native American, but we never talked about his heritage. He claimed to make his living playing cards: He bought land, owned rental properties, and always carried a thick wad of cash.

He talked about collecting social security. Knocking men out with a single punch. Hiding money. Buying homes with no loans. His best friend was rumored to be a mafia boss. He stayed out most nights. He belonged to the country club, played golf, and hosted late-night card games.

But what went on was never discussed. None of it made sense to me as a kid. We looked rich, but we lived without any of the comforts that should have come with it.

We walked on eggshells.
Don't ask.
Don't talk.
Don't upset him.

From the outside, we looked like we had it all. Nice house. Nice cars. Country club life.

But inside, it was cold.
Bleak.

There was no beauty. No peace. Just the illusion of abundance.

And that's all it was.
An illusion.

As Jehovah's Witnesses, we didn't celebrate birthdays or Christmas. That meant no gifts. No new clothes. No shared joy. And no one was taking us shopping just because we needed something.

Money was my father's god. He spent it on clubs, cards, cars, and control. But not on us.

I wasn't asking for luxury. I was a lonely girl with no friends, wearing out-of-style clothes that didn't fit. It was cruel to have plenty of money and choose to withhold it.

And I knew better than to ask. To even believe there might be money left over for something I needed was an offense. The unspoken message was clear:

You don't matter.
What you want is stupid.
What you need is irrelevant.

My mother was treated the same. So she didn't protect me. Fight for me. She didn't do much of anything.

She stayed home, but didn't clean, didn't work in the yard, and cooked only the easiest meals. Hamburger Helper was her go-to. We ate it constantly. To this day, I've never bought it. I can still taste it. The house itself was full of mold and roaches.

As an adult, when I was tested for allergies, the doctor asked if I'd grown up around roaches. My results were off the charts.

That house wasn't safety, comfort, or security. It was just a house.

Spiritually, it was isolating too. Through our religion, my mother taught me that everyone outside our faith was bad. Worldly. Off-limits.

We weren't to associate with anyone unless we were witnessing to them. We were meant to remain separate. From everything. From everyone.

My father believed everyone was a sucker. He laughed when people lost money. Boasted about conning people out of something. Giving to the poor, to a church, to anyone in need, he saw all of it as weaknesses.

He especially hated women. All women.

To him, they were meant to be dominated. Used. Good for nothing else.

It was understood in our home: Men have many women. That's just what men do.

My mother taught me to fear the world.
My father taught me to despise it.

The only place colder than our house was the Kingdom Hall.

Cult

Most teenagers go through a phase where they're embarrassed by their parents. I've worked with teens for over twenty-five years, it's normal.

A girl might cringe when her mom speaks, even if all she says is, "Hi, honey." You'll hear it, "Mom?!"—like breathing in public is a mortal sin.

But that phase usually passes. The girl grows into a woman who sees her mother as a hero, a role model. Her best friend.

I knew even then: That was never going to be my mother and me.

There was a heaviness in our home. A quiet sadness. But the feeling that haunted me most was guilt. Crushing, constant, paralyzing guilt.

For what, I had no idea.

My father and brother spent most of their time together. If Dad wasn't playing cards, he was playing golf, and my brother went with him.

The Struggle for Self-Worth

I wasn't invited.

I stayed home with my mother. Which meant one thing: we were going to the Kingdom Hall of Jehovah's Witnesses. Our week followed a pattern.

Go to school because it was required. But don't make friends with "worldly people." Don't participate in their activities. Just go to school. Come home. Prepare for the Hall.

A central teaching in the Jehovah's Witness community is the need to remain separate from the world.

This is known as *separation orientation*—the idea that believers should avoid entanglement with worldly events, relationships, or media. Researchers Lyman Kellstedt and Corwin Smidt have written about this in relation to high-control religious groups.[3]

In the Watchtower article, *"Will You Follow Jehovah's Loving Guidance?,"* believers are admonished not to follow after the crowd or allow nonbelievers to influence them, especially through visual or written media.[4]

Another publication warns members to "avoid them [nonbelievers] as we would a poison or poisonous snake."[5]

My life revolved around the Hall. We attended services every Tuesday and Thursday night, where we were trained to witness effectively. Saturday mornings were for door-to-door ministry. The elders divided the city into territories and assigned us to different neighborhoods.

Before heading out, we'd stop at the Hall bookstore to buy copies of *The Watchtower* and *Awake!* magazines, along with any other literature we wanted to sell.

Then we'd break into groups of four, pile into someone's car, and head out.

We knocked in pairs.
Always in pairs.

I dreaded the knock. Not theirs. Mine. I was terrified I'd knock on the door of someone I knew from school. I was already an outcast. This would just be more ammunition for their cruelty.

I have memories of those mornings. My mom holding my hand. The other women chatting in the car. I don't remember any men. Just mothers, daughters, and sadness.

They would talk about their lives, their struggles, their families. Sometimes, their words turned into tears.

I was too young to understand why.
I just knew they were hurting.
And then there was the rock.

In New Orleans, many of the homes we visited were shotgun houses, narrow and long. You could stand at the front door, fire a shotgun, and the bullet would fly straight through to the back without hitting a wall. Families often stayed in the back, so they couldn't hear a knock at the front.

That was my job. As a little girl, I was assigned to carry a rock. If no one answered the front door, I'd run down the side of the house and knock on the middle wall with my rock. Hard enough to get their attention.

That sound—stone against wood—was part of my childhood.

CHAPTER THREE:
FINDING FAITH IN UNLIKELY PLACES

There were moments I felt proud getting up at 7 a.m. on a Saturday to meet at the Kingdom Hall for my assignment.

Arriving by 8, there was a flicker of excitement. I believed I was doing what God wanted by bringing new Jehovah's Witnesses into the faith.

The Kingdom Hall was plain. Rows of chairs. A podium. A bookstore. No crosses. No stained glass. No artwork. They believed all of Christendom was pagan, full of idols and false worship. Now, as an adult, I've come to appreciate symbols not as idols, but as reminders. Reminders that God is near.

On Thursday nights, we were taught how to handle objections at the door. I'd silently beg, Oh God, please don't let anyone challenge me.

I marked verses in my Jehovah's Witness Bible, *The New World Translation of the Holy Scriptures*, and practiced my delivery. But it was never about love. Never about the redemptive power of Jesus. Never about grace. The Bible's central story—redemption, rescue, grace— was buried under rules.

The words "God loves you" were never part of my assignment. Still, I was drawn to Jesus. Even as a child, I noticed: Christmas was about Him. Easter was about Him. Our calendar centered on His birth. Other churches seemed to revolve around Him. In the Jehovah's Witness teachings, Jesus was acknowledged as the Son of God—but never as God Himself. The Trinity was considered pagan. The idea of Jesus being both fully God and fully man was dismissed. The cross, too, was rejected—seen not as a symbol of hope but as idolatry. They said Jesus was hung on a tree, not crucified. His virgin birth, death, and resurrection were mentioned but never explained.

The concept of grace was absent. Salvation, I learned, was earned through works. That confused me. Deeply. But I kept searching. The Lord's Prayer, for example, meant something to me. Even though we rarely talked about Jesus, His words in that prayer gave me comfort. "Our Father in heaven, hallowed be your name…"

It seemed simple. Beautiful. Every night, I would read it. Recite it. I didn't understand it all, but it reached something in me.

Sundays followed a rhythm. One hour of teaching from an elder, not a seminary-trained pastor, just a member assigned to speak. We'd sing a single hymn played from a record. Then came a second hour. A study of *The Watchtower* and *Awake!* magazines.

The teachings were standardized, written and scheduled by the Governing Body in New York. Not scripture. Just rules. Immersed in a bath of rules and guidelines, regular pioneers were expected to evangelize 600 hours a year. Auxiliary pioneers gave 30 hours in a month. If you failed to meet your quota, the elders would meet with you. You'd be reminded of your responsibility. Their expectations. The price of falling short.

Some sermons terrified me. I remember one elder shouting from the platform: "If we tell you to jump up and lie down on the floor—you must do it!" His finger pointed straight into the crowd. I felt it pointed straight at me. My mom whispered, "What an incredible speaker."

I remember thinking: Shouldn't we ask why?

> The guilt never stopped.
> Never enough.
> Never good enough.
> Never safe.

It wasn't just about religion. It was the confusion of my mother's rules. The absence of my father's. And the silence in between.

Scripture was sprinkled in, but even that felt filtered. Ancient scholars or respected theologians did not shape the *New World Translation*. It had been rewritten behind closed doors by men who believed their interpretation was the only truth. I didn't know that yet. But something deep inside me sensed it wasn't right.

Early on, I began questioning what I was being taught. One Sunday, we read from Matthew 22:34–40:

"'Teacher, which is the greatest commandment in the Law?'

Jesus replied: "'You must love Jehovah your God with your whole heart, your whole soul, and your whole mind. This is the greatest and first commandment. The second is like it: You must love your neighbor as yourself. On these two commandments hang the whole Law and the Prophets.'" (NWT)

I was stunned.

If these are the two greatest commandments…

Then why are there so many rules?

So many laws? So many heavy expectations?
It didn't make sense. And then we read Matthew 5:17:

"Do not think I came to destroy the Law or the Prophets. I came not to destroy, but to fulfill." (NWT)

That was it.

That verse opened something in me. Jesus didn't come to add to the burden. He came to carry it. He fulfilled the Law.
Who was this Jesus?
They couldn't explain Him away. The deeper I looked, the more I saw that the weight they placed on followers was never His doing.

It was cruel.
It was not of God.

And I began to thank God daily for revealing Himself to me.

"Come to me, all who are weary and burdened, and I will give you rest… My yoke is easy, and my burden is light." (Matthew 11:28–30 NIV)

I didn't find Him at the front of the Hall. I found Him in the pages of Scripture, in the very words buried beneath the rhetoric.

"So if the Son sets you free, you will be free indeed." (John 8:36 NIV)

Free indeed.

CHAPTER FOUR:
INNER TURMOIL & TORTURE

The inner turmoil is hard to explain. You're told the world is evil. Stay separate. Yet God gave me love for people, talents to grow, and a longing to learn and give.

At home, I lived under constant guilt and shame. My mother made me feel like I was never enough. The organization taught that self-belief was sinful. Then there was my father pushing me to excel in sports I wasn't supposed to participate in.

It felt like torture.
I was aggressive.
Athletic.

Wherever we moved, my dad enrolled me in something new even though Jehovah's Witnesses discouraged organized sports. My mom disapproved, but allowed it.

No one drove me to practice.
No one came to my games.

I'd overhear them rave about my brother. Every game attended, every achievement praised. It wasn't just confusing.

It was cruel.

In every sport I joined, I stood out.

Coaches noticed.
Teammates noticed.
Everyone noticed.
Except my parents.

Dad always had a country club membership. Every weekend, he and my brother were there, golfing. He said it was important. Said the poker tables were full of rich guys. Easy marks. "There's no better mark than a rich man with a bad poker face."

He'd come home bragging about his take, a wad of cash folded in his back pocket. Cash was king. He worshiped his king. Dominating the table, taking from the weak. That was his religion. His sacrament.

I don't know whether it was my Native American heritage or just bad luck, but my acne started young, and it was bad. My dad and his brothers had pockmarked faces too. We never saw doctors. That kind of help wasn't for people like us. I know all teenagers struggle with feeling different.

It wasn't just the acne. It was the same clothes every day. The shame of never fitting in. Then the weight gain that followed a violent event in my teens.

When the country club opened tennis signups for juniors, my dad enrolled me.

And like always, I was excited. My mom gave me her usual look of disgust.

Then came "the speech":

> "You know the elders say we're not supposed to participate in
> organized sports.
> Being competitive isn't what Jehovah wants.
> You'll be around worldly people by choice."

The speech worked every time, except when my dad said I could do something.

> Sports were my reprieve.
> A moment of fun.
> Time with friends.
> I stood out, special.

The first day of practice, the coach had us run a drill.

Hit over the net. Rotate to the back of the line. Miss, and you're out. Last one standing wins.

I'd never played tennis before. But something inside me locked in:

Don't miss.
Make them miss.
I will not be beat.

It boiled in my chest. I would not lose. I would be the last one standing.

And I was.

To the coach's amazement, I beat the returning players. I'd never picked up a racket before, but I loved the game. And I was good at it.

The coach started spending more time with me, coaching me more than the others.

I quickly became the number one player.

One Saturday, after my dad and brother finished golfing at the country club, they came to pick me up. My coach pulled my dad aside. He told him I was special. If my dad supported it, he could develop me into a world-class player.

I couldn't believe what I was hearing. Two grown men talking about *me.* My dad's eyes met mine. He smiled and nodded.

For the first time in my life, I felt loved.

Chosen.
Not tolerated. Not overlooked.
I was wanted. Seen.

It wasn't just that I was good at something.

It was that someone noticed.

Sure, I was excited about winning tournaments. But the deeper thrill was this: My dad was proud of me.

He smiled *because of me.*

And for a moment, that was everything.

They didn't say much in front of me, but I knew they talked behind closed doors. So I just kept practicing. I was getting better every day. Winning team drills. Making friends. I loved every minute I spent at the country club after school.

This must be what normal feels like.
Acceptance.

Then I started entering local tournaments and winning those too. But with every win, my mom grew colder.
The remarks began:

"You don't look like you belong out there."
"Look at your opponent. She knows what she's doing."

The same curled lip. The same smirk. As if she enjoyed saying it.
When I lost my first match, I was crushed.
Then she drove it in:

"I watched her warmup and thought, 'You're in trouble.'
She's way out of your league."

Then came the guilt:

"If you keep playing, we'll talk to the elders.
This isn't what Jehovah wants from you."

And that was it.

She won.

The shame set in—*What was I doing? I embarrassed myself. I went against God.*
At the next practice, I said my back hurt. Coach told me to rest up for the weekend tournament.
Every day that week, I sat on the sidelines while my friends practiced. And every day, I knew: *I didn't belong there anymore.*

The fun was gone.
The belonging was gone.

Saturday came.
My dad bounced around the house, loading the car, excited.

And I felt sick.

They all wanted me to win—Coach, my team, my dad. But if I played,

God would hate me.
And I couldn't live with that.

As match time approached, I made my decision. I had to lose. It was the only way out. I threw every point. When my opponent messed up, I got angry. *Don't make this harder*, I thought. Let's just end it.

When it was over, I gathered my things and walked toward the parking lot. No eye contact. No goodbyes.

"Hey," my dad called behind me.

I kept walking.

"Hey," he repeated.

I stopped and turned.

"Why did you quit?"

I said nothing.

"Why did you quit?" he asked again.

Still nothing.
Then he shoved me against the car and hit me. I fell to the ground.

But something rose up in me.
This man I feared.
Loved.
Hated.

Now standing over me, yelling.

I got up.

And I hit back.

Yelling.
Swinging.

He pulled back his fist. The same fist known for dropping grown men with one punch. Then a voice behind him: "Stop!" A stranger.

His rage turned to embarrassment. He stopped. We got in the car.

We never spoke of tennis again.

The Bear

It's not normal for a child to feel like a bear lives in the house. But that's how it was.

Imagine this: You're walking through the woods, just taking a stroll. The sun peeks through the trees, scattering light like glitter on the ground. It's warm, but the breeze cools your skin. Birdsong in the distance. The trees rustle like they're waving to you as you pass underneath.

You feel at peace.
Then off in the distance,
you hear a grunt.
It grows into a growl.
You freeze.

You don't see anything yet, but you know. Your body knows.

The ringing in your ears.
The hair rising on your arms.
The thunder of your heartbeat.
You strain to see it.
You try to listen harder.
You don't just hear it.
You *feel* it.

The only question is: *Will it pass by? Or will it charge?*

So you stay still.
Don't move.
Don't breathe.
Don't make eye contact.
Maybe it won't notice you.

That's what it's like when a bear lives in your house.

That's what it was like for me.

School

School wasn't a break from the tension.

It was just another place I didn't belong.

I was different. Not just felt it, was it.

I wasn't allowed to have friends. Couldn't participate in school activities. Teachers didn't know what to do with me and some seemed annoyed by me. During Christmas songs or holiday crafts, I was sent into the hallway.

No birthday parties.
No gifts.
No celebrations.
Not mine.
Not anyone else's.

I wore the same few clothes over and over. My acne was bad. I was an easy target.

The bullying didn't stop with students. Even teachers joined in.

That stung the worst.

Boys made crude jokes and whispered nicknames I couldn't quite hear, but I knew they were about me. And still, no one came to rescue me.

In fact, every part of life kept getting worse.

The Bible and the Blind Woman

But even then, a flicker of light came through.

One afternoon while going door to door, I knocked on a screen door in a poor Black neighborhood. A woman's voice called from inside, "What do you want?"

I introduced myself with the usual Jehovah's Witness routine and she surprised me. She said she was blind and couldn't read the Bible.

Then she asked: "Would you read it to me?"

From that day on, I visited every week after school.

Her house was old, run-down, crawling with roaches. They'd skitter over my shoes, crawl into my bag. And still—I *loved* going. I'd sit at her feet and read Scripture. Sometimes we'd talk about it. Other times, we just talked. It was the first time in a long time I felt… welcome.

She babysat her grandchildren. I still remember her voice: "Go get my switch."

They'd stand still while she swatted them. They respected her and loved her.

One week, I couldn't go. I asked my mom to go in my place.

When she came back, I asked, "How did it go?"

"Fine," she said. "She likes you. Said you make the Bible easy to understand. It's because you're simple. Like her."

There it was again.
The bite.
That same sharp edge.
Saved for me.

But this one felt like betrayal. Because I never saw the woman again. I don't know what happened.

I just know she never asked me to come back.

That silence said everything.

Rape

As a Jehovah's Witness, you weren't allowed to associate with anyone outside the faith. That meant no real social life. Even among other Witnesses, there was an air of suspicion. If someone did something wrong, someone else was expected to report it.

The innocence of childhood—the silliness, the belly laughs, the safety of friendship—was rare.

I think of my own children now. I've watched my son and daughter play and laugh and just *be*. That kind of joy was foreign to me. I had moments that *looked* like childhood but none that felt safe.

Even later in life, I felt embarrassed by how little I knew. Simple things. Everyday things. I'd missed them all. But the moment I truly began to know God, things shifted.

He gave me a vision once. Something gentle, healing.

I saw a grandfather in a kitchen, watching his granddaughter play. She was lost in her world, and then she noticed the cookie jar on the counter. She looked around, didn't see him, and took a cookie she wasn't supposed to have.

> He saw it all.
> And he smiled.
> Not in anger.
> Not in judgment.
> He loved her.

He was a little sad she'd spoil her dinner, but she was still his joy. Still the most delightful thing he'd ever seen.

That was the moment I began to understand who God really is. Not an angry overseer, waiting to punish. Not like the god I grew up with.

That god—my mother's god—was always watching, always disappointed, and I believed I was his easiest target. I lived under his glare. And under hers.

So when a Jehovah's Witness friend invited me to a sleepover, it felt like a gift. A bit of normal. She'd invited another girl too, someone I didn't know well. I remember feeling excited. Included.

> Her older brother was 17.
> We were 14.

That night we all watched movies in the living room until people started going off to bed. One by one, they left. Until it was just the two of us.

He was cute. I liked the attention. I wasn't used to it, and it made me feel… wanted.

When he kissed me, I felt butterflies. But that wasn't where the night ended. And it wasn't butterflies I remembered when it was over.

> He asked, "Want a drink?"
> "Sure."

He poured me a Coke. I remember thinking how kind that was. I'd never seen my dad serve anyone before, certainly not a girl. I didn't know guys did that.

I took a sip and something felt off.
He quickly said, "Drink it. You'll love it."

I liked him. I wanted him to like me. So I drank it. All of it.
The next morning, I woke up… disoriented.

My head was foggy.
My body felt wrong.
Dizzy.
Weak.

And I was lying on the stairs.
I could hear his mother in the kitchen, cooking breakfast. I panicked.

What happened?
Did she see me?
Why was I here?

I tried to stand, but my legs were shaky. My stomach turned. And then panic.

I wasn't wearing any underwear.
I froze.

My body felt like it belonged to someone else. I spotted my panties at the bottom of the stairs. I grabbed them and ran.

Upstairs.
Straight to the friend's room.
Woke her up.

I tried to explain what little I could remember. She listened, kind of, but not really.

When I told her what I remembered, she said, "We have to tell the elders."

I begged her not to. "Please," I whispered. "I'm scared." But she didn't even look at me.

Looking back, I don't think she was being cruel. She was doing what we were all trained to do. Jehovah's Witnesses don't cover each other in hard times.

We report.
Interrogate.
Look for what's wrong in people.

I knew she'd go to the elders. I called my mom. She picked me up. We said nothing.

When we got home, I went straight to my room. That night, she came in and said,

"We have a meeting with the elders tomorrow."

That was it.
No questions.
No comfort.
Just disgust.
The bear was in the room again.

The fear didn't just sit in my chest; it tore through me. A pain so sharp it burned.

I didn't have language for what had happened. But I knew something awful had. And I knew this:

I was guilty.
I didn't deserve to be loved.
Not by my mother.
Not by God.

The next day, we walked into the Kingdom Hall. Empty except for the three elders sitting in a row.

They didn't smile. Just motioned for me to sit in a single chair across from them. My mom sat off to the side. Between me and them. Close enough to feel.

They started with soft questions:

"Did you like him?"
"Did you find him attractive?"
"Did he kiss you?"

The bear was back.

Not pacing the edges this time.
He charged.
The foulness of his breath.
His teeth gnawing at my spirit.

Tearing through what was left of my safety, my voice, my worth.

I was a child, already wounded. And I was being devoured by those who should have defended me. I was terrified.

The questions got darker.

I braced for worse.

One by one, the elders pressed in with questions:

"Did he touch you?"
"Where?"
"Did you like it?"
"Did you have sex?"
"Who took your panties off? Him or you?"

I looked at my mom, silently pleading for help. I didn't even know what they were asking. Didn't know what to say.

I was embarrassed.
Exposed.
Ashamed.
Frozen.

She didn't come to my defense. Didn't say a word. Just stared back at me, her lips turned slightly upward, like she was... amused.

I felt like I was going to pass out. But no one was coming to help me.

No one.

I couldn't answer their questions.

I was frozen.

One of them finally told me to leave the room so they could speak with my mother privately.

I tried to stand.

My legs wouldn't move at first. They felt stiff and numb, like I'd been sitting in ice water.

We got back in the car.
My mom didn't look at me.

After a long silence, she said,

"You're going to be disfellowshipped."

I didn't even know what that meant.
She explained it coldly.

"If the elders decide to disfellowship you, no one is allowed to speak to you. Except the people who live in your home. Not until you're reinstated. Usually after six months.

You have to earn it.

Attend every meeting.
Follow every rule.
Prove you're worthy.

It didn't feel like discipline.

It felt like exile.

We got home, and I went straight to my room.

As usual, my father wasn't there. After a while, I heard the back door open. Then close.

The bear was back.

I could feel him before I saw him.

My heart started racing.
My breath caught.
Yelling came from the kitchen.

Then, in an instant, my door slammed open.
He burst in, grabbed me, and threw me against the bed.
The wooden slats underneath snapped from the force.

He hit me.
Yelled at me.
Called me a slut.

I curled into a ball, trying to protect my face. My ribs. My stomach.

Then, it stopped.

I looked up from the floor, He was sitting on the edge of the broken bed.

Crying.

Crying?

I didn't understand.

I'd seen him cry when our dog died. But never over a person.

Never over me.

I stood stunned.

Walked over.
Sat next to him.
I put my arm around him.
Patted his back.
He stood up.

Left the room.
And we never spoke of it again.

Looking back, it still feels unreal.

I was fourteen.
Already afraid of men.
Didn't even understand what sex was.

And I believed, truly believed, that God already hated me.

That everyone did.
It changes you.

Now, as an older woman, I realize how sleazy those men were to ask me those questions. Looking back, I believe they took a kind of satisfaction in it. That thought makes me sick.

What devastates me even more is knowing my mother allowed it.

She sat there.
She watched.
And she let it happen.

The people who were supposed to protect me didn't.

I was taken advantage of by a boy who knew I was vulnerable. When it all came to light, his father blamed me. My mother blamed me.

So of course I believed I was guilty. I thought: *What's wrong with me?*

It was Sunday morning, and we were off to the Kingdom Hall. As always, it was just my mother and me. Dad and my brother were at the country club. No one mentioned what was about to happen. We all acted like it was just another day.

But I knew it wasn't.

I had that feeling again.

There was a bear in the room.

I couldn't see him, but I could feel him.

We walked in. We didn't speak to anyone. That wasn't unusual. A quick "Good morning," then straight to our seats.

But this Sunday was different. We sat in the back row. Not our usual spot.

The service began with a prayer. Then a song played from a record. An elder stepped forward to give the talk. (They're not called sermons.)

These talks were hard to follow. Maybe it was because I was fourteen. Maybe it was because they lasted an hour. Maybe it was because the men giving them weren't trained speakers. It was just their turn.

Over the years, I developed an uncanny ability to disappear inside myself. I could zone out for the entire service, escaping to some other place in my mind. It became a survival skill.

The talk ended. We stood for another song. Then sat down again for the *Watchtower* study.

This was the second hour.

The elder would read the magazine aloud, pausing to ask questions. A few people raised their hands to answer. Always the same ones. Every week.

It was predictable.
Mechanical.
Mind-numbing.

But this Sunday was different.

And it was time.

The elder closed the *Watchtower*, looked out at the congregation, and then looked directly at me.

He said:

"It has been decided by the elders that Dena Evans has had conduct unbecoming of a Christian. She is now disfellowshipped. You are not to speak to her at any time until we deem her repentant and reinstate her."

I could hear my heart pounding in my ears.
I sat frozen as gasps echoed through the room.

Then came the slow turn of heads. All of them looking at me.

I dropped my gaze, afraid to move.
I could feel the bear breathing on my neck.
I wanted to crumble.

But I stood for the closing song.
When it was over, we slipped out the back door without a word.

The Weight of Blame

Every week followed the same pattern, three meetings at the Kingdom Hall. While I was disfellowshipped, I no longer had to go door to door on Saturday mornings. Inside the Hall, no one spoke to me.

That wasn't really new. I hadn't had friends before. I'd always felt invisible. Now, though, it was official. My shame had a spotlight.

The beliefs I carried—that I was guilty, ruined, unlovable—felt carved in stone. School didn't offer any relief. I stopped trying to be part of anything.

The weight came on. My hair stayed wild and became a shield to hide my face. I was still there, physically.

At school.
At the Hall.

But mentally, I was retreating.

Shrinking.

Years later, I found words for what I'd lived through.

In an article that studied the long-term impact of shunning among the Jehovah's Witnesses, the authors wrote:

"Results suggest shunning has a long-term, detrimental effect on mental health, job possibilities, and life satisfaction. Problems are amplified in female former members due to heavy themes of sexism and patriarchal narratives... Feelings of loneliness, loss of control, and worthlessness are also common after leaving. The culture of informing on other members... leads to a continued sense of distrust and suspicion long after leaving."[6]

Back then, I didn't know how to say any of that.
But my soul felt every bit of it.

Eventually, the six-month sentence ended. The announcement was made—I'd been reinstated.

A few people came over to say "Congratulations."

I remember wondering: *For what?*

CHAPTER FIVE:
CHOOSING TO LIVE

Breaking Point

Turning sixteen didn't mean anything special. Jehovah's Witnesses don't celebrate birthdays. No cake, no gifts, no acknowledgment of the day you were born. At least not in our home.

I wouldn't even remember that I was sixteen if it weren't for the event.

That morning, while I was getting ready for school, my dad walked into my room and said flatly, "I'm leaving your mother. We're getting a divorce."

That was it.
No warning.
No discussion.
Just the words.

Honestly, it wasn't a surprise. He was never home. There were always other women.

Then he added, "I'm not happy with your mom."

And I, without thinking, replied, "I guess you need to be happy."

That sentence, those seven words, set off a chain reaction I couldn't have predicted.

Not "I'm leaving."
Not "We're getting a divorce."
But "I guess you need to be happy."

He told my mom later that even I understood he deserved happiness.

From that moment on, she didn't just dislike me.

She hated me.

She'd never had coping skills. Never took responsibility for anything. But now, this was her death blow.

> I became her target.
> Her words were colder.
> Her glances, sharper.

She only spoke to me when necessary, and always with disdain.

The only relief came when her anger turned on someone else: my father, the other women, the world. I know it's awful to say, but those moments felt like reprieve.

I thought maybe, just maybe, if I could comfort her, she would see me differently.

> As an ally.
> As a daughter.

But her behavior only spiraled.

Most mornings, I woke up wondering if the bear was in the house.

> Most days, it was.

One morning, thinking she was still asleep, I opened the door to find a stranger standing there.

> A man.
> Holding her up.

"Is this your mother?" he asked.

She was limp in his arms, drunk. He'd found her in a ditch.

He carried her in, and I cleaned her up. I made her coffee, something warm. Familiar. Comforting.

She took a sip and hurled the cup across the floor.

"It has sugar," she hissed. "I hate sugar in my coffee!"

> I scrambled to make her another.

Some nights, she didn't come home at all. I stayed up and watched my younger brother. I always did.

Then came the night she staggered in smelling like liquor, not fully drunk, but off.

She sat down and started talking.

"I met a man," she said. "He was gorgeous. He'd never look at you."

She smiled, a smirk really. Her eyes darted up at me, sharp and gleaming.

Daggers.
I froze.
The bear was rising again.

But maybe she just needed someone.

Maybe she needed me?

And then she started describing what they'd done.

Not vaguely. Not delicately.
Details. *Too many.*
It was sickening. My stomach turned.

Why was she telling me this?
She had never explained sex to me.

Not how it worked.
Not what it meant.

Not in any way that made sense or sounded safe.

Even though I'd already been raped, I still didn't understand what had happened to me.

But here she was, telling me about her sexual encounter. Like it was funny. Normal.

I was disgusted.
Things only got worse.

My dad had moved in with the other woman. He avoided the house, which meant we were alone with her. All the time.

Then one afternoon, I got off the bus after another awful day at school—more bullying, more whispers, more shame. I walked home expecting to see her, like always. But the house was quiet.

I headed to the kitchen for a snack.
That's when I saw the note on the counter.
I don't remember how it started.
I don't remember how it ended.

Just one line:

*"Satan has won. I'm going to kill myself—
but first, I'll kill my children."*

Honestly, my first thought was: Where is she? The note was still on the counter. The words echoing in my head.

She wanted to kill us.
Was she still here?
In the house?

I looked outside and the car was gone. That brought a flicker of relief. She wasn't home. But where was she? Could she come back any minute?

Then I saw my little brother walking up the driveway after school. What do I do?

Do I tell him?
No. No way.
But I had to get in touch with Dad.

He was never around, always off with his new girlfriend, usually traveling out of the country. I wasn't sure he'd answer. But this time, he did. I told him about the note.

"I don't know where she is," I said. "But she's not here. And she said..."

He came over immediately.

A few minutes later, the phone rang. It was Mom.

She was at the beach.

She said she needed time to think. Said she'd be home in a few days. I let her talk. Asked how long she'd be gone. She repeated, "A few days." Calm. Cold.

I tried to hand the phone to Dad so he could talk to her.

He wouldn't take it.
We hung up.

That was all he needed.

He folded the note, put it in his pocket, and said, "She'll be back in a few days. Take care of your brother until then." Then he left.

Just like that.

Sure, I was old enough to stay home. Old enough to cook. Old enough to watch over my little brother. But I'd just found a note saying my mother wanted to kill us. And no one—no one—checked to see if we were okay.

Not my mother.
Not my father.

Something shifted in me that day. Something deep.
I realized: No one is coming.

My mother isn't well.
My father isn't protecting us.

I'm done.

Something in my spirit shut down.
No tears.
No questions.

Just the numb resolve of someone who stopped caring.
The first thing I noticed:

The bear was gone.

For the first time in a long time, I didn't feel fear in the house. No dread. No waiting for the door to slam or the air to shift. I felt something else.

Anger.

You're crazy. You're selfish.

I didn't whisper it.
I thought it.
A declaration.
And I meant it.

I was done caring. Done waiting for someone to come protect me. Done believing I was powerless.

I didn't know where I'd go or how I'd get out, but I knew this: I was leaving. Not that day, not the next but I was already halfway gone.

I started working out. My face cleared. My body changed.

I took what little money I had and bought myself clothes that made me feel more like a person. I started to rise.

Whatever had broken inside me, it also cracked something open.

A voice.
A will.
A sense that maybe I could live differently.

I couldn't name it at the time, but I had chosen something.

Not rebellion.
Not revenge.

I chose to live.

SECTION TWO:

FINDING THE LIGHT

CHAPTER SIX:
LOVE & HOPE

Bright Spots and Flickers of Hope

One of those seasons came when we moved to California. During my childhood, there were rare moments when someone noticed me. A teacher or adult would say something kind, recognize a talent, or go out of their way to encourage me. Those flickers of light stayed with me.

This happened before everything fell apart. I remember it clearly, because it was one of the first times I felt strong. Everything was different there: the way people talked, the way school worked, even the way they thought. I wasn't used to it, but it felt new in a good way.

At school, free expression and creativity were encouraged. Art and sports had always been my outlets, and for once, both were celebrated. When I painted, teachers praised me.

> They liked me.
> They noticed me.
> That was new.

My mom stopped going to the Kingdom Hall, and life got a little looser. Lighter. We had more freedom than usual.

As always, my dad signed me up for a sport. This time, a track club. I was still in elementary school. My mom dropped me off on the first day of practice, and I had no idea what to expect.

The coach didn't waste time.

"Run a mile around the track," he said. "If you stop or talk to anyone, you're off the team."

I'd never run a mile before. But I did it. When I finished, proud of myself, I walked up to him and said, "I'm done."

He barely looked at me.

"Now run sprints down the middle of the track. Walk back. Sprint again. Don't stop. Don't talk. I'll tell you when to stop."

It was the hardest thing I had ever done but I didn't stop.

Later that evening, back at the house, I stood in the kitchen while Mom made Hamburger Helper.

"I don't think I want to do track anymore," I said.

Without looking up, she replied, "That's fine. I knew you'd quit. You're a quitter."

Her words lit something in me.

> Anger.
> Fire.
> Resolve.

I went back the next day. And the next. I trained hard.

> Got faster.
> Stronger.
> Better.

And for once, they noticed. Both of them.

My parents came to my meets. They sat in the stands, cheering me on. I kept winning and eventually made it all the way to the AAU National Meet in California. I placed second in the 220-meter race.

> I was proud of myself.
> I had friends.
> I felt happy.

But like most bright spots in my life, that season didn't last.

> We moved again.
> Back to Louisiana.

My mother returned to the Kingdom Hall.

> And I faded into the background.
> Again.

The Scent of Belonging

Before Aunt Nell, I didn't know what it felt like to be cherished.

She called me "Sugar" and wrapped me in full-bodied hugs. When I spoke, she leaned in, smiled, really smiled, and listened like what I had to say mattered. She said I was smart. Talented. Seen.

I watched everything she did: how she treated her husband, how she cooked, how she moved through a room like light. She was always doing something for someone else. She radiated joy. She radiated love.

Aunt Nell was also an artist. She taught lessons in a little building on a bluff above the Caddo River in Glenwood, Arkansas. She loved to paint. And she taught me to love it too. She showed me how to sketch, how to prepare a canvas, and how to mix colors. I can still remember the scent of linseed oil the moment I opened the door to her studio.

That smell meant peace.
It meant belonging.

It was a little piece of heaven.

Quiet, creative, sacred.

Uncle Tommy, her husband, was just as special. He loved science, especially astronomy. We'd sit and talk for hours. He'd explain the stars, the laws of nature, how science and faith could coexist. He didn't just talk; he listened. He'd say, "That's a great question," and mean it.

Once, I asked him, "If you dig down to find older rocks and fossils, and the earth keeps building new layers, does that mean the earth is getting bigger?"

He didn't laugh. He didn't dismiss it. He looked at me with bright eyes and said, "That's a wonderful question. You're a thinking person. Let me read a little and get back to you."

No one had ever said that to me before. I was a child in a house that looked normal from the outside. But it wasn't. A child who'd never been hugged. Never heard the words "I love you." A child who'd been told I was silly, who believed I didn't matter.

Aunt Nell and Uncle Tommy changed that.

I carried their kindness home like a treasure. One I had to hide the moment I closed the front door.

When I got home, my parents mocked them.

Dad said they were poor and stupid. Mom said Aunt Nell was worldly and that she'd be destroyed in Armageddon. I couldn't believe it. These were the kindest, most life-giving people I'd ever met.

Sure, they drank from mason jars and watched a TV with no channels. But they grew vegetables and canned their own food. They gave generously. They thought deeply. They laughed freely. Everything my parents called foolish, I found profound.

I told my mom I wanted to visit again. "She's my sister!" she snapped, like that somehow justified her disdain.

But I knew the truth. Aunt Nell and Uncle Tommy had shown me something beautiful. And I tucked it away inside. This. *This* is the kind of life I wanted: kind, creative, joyful, curious, full of love.

I only saw them three times growing up. But when someone truly sees you, it doesn't take many moments to make a mark.

Love leaves a lasting imprint.
Mentoring isn't always about lessons.

Sometimes it's about seeing a soul and honoring it.

Stranger with the Blue Eyes

After the incident at sixteen, I made up my mind I was getting out, somehow, some way. My mother still had fits of rage, but the bear was gone. I didn't care anymore. One day I "borrowed" a shirt of hers. Washed it. Forgot to put it back on a hanger. She stormed into my room and threw it at me. "How dare you! This is mine. Don't touch my stuff."

I didn't flinch.

She looked shocked that I showed no emotion. I had changed. And it felt good.

I was barely getting through school. As a Jehovah's Witness, college wasn't allowed. School was only a requirement of the government. Our future was marriage and children within the faith. So I skipped whenever I could, took easy business electives, and did just enough to pass. I graduated, but no one celebrated.

I needed to work. I had no plan, no vision, no support. I overheard someone say you could make good money hanging wallpaper, so I went to a job site and asked if they needed help. They said yes. I learned, bought supplies, printed business cards, and started working.

The work wasn't hard, but it was hot in the Louisiana summers, cold, wet, and muddy in the winters. Still, it got me out of the house. I had one friend, Mimi. She was older and still lived with her mom. She made me laugh. We were both Jehovah's Witnesses. Dating options were limited, and we were both restless. I'd just turned eighteen. I had seldom been away from my mother overnight.

One night I said, "It's June. The water in Florida will be warm. Let's go tomorrow. We can sleep in the car." She agreed. At sunrise, we left. It felt wild. We knew we'd be in trouble with the elders when we got back. But for once, we didn't care.

We arrived midday. The sun was high. The breeze was soft. The waves rolled in gentle and bright. Freedom tasted brand new. I remember thinking, no one looking at me knows how big this is. Most people take this kind of freedom for granted. Waking up without fear, without shame. But I had lived with abandonment inside the same house as my family. There's a cruelty to being unloved by those who are supposed to love you. You learn to survive alone. And still, something in the ocean air whispered:

"I see you. I love you.
I have something good in store for you."

Mimi told a couple of Jehovah's Witness friends, and they found us on the beach. They had a hotel room and invited us to stay. That night we went out.

A beach bar.
Pool tables.
Music.
Laughter.

Jehovah's Witnesses didn't do this kind of thing, but here we were.

The night before, I'd had a dream. I saw a pair of deep blue eyes in a dim room. I couldn't see the face, just the eyes full of kindness. Full of love.

That night, we were playing pool. In walked a guy with the bluest eyes I'd ever seen. "Can we play?" he asked. I don't think I answered, just smiled. We talked all night. It was electric.

He was from Louisiana too, just a couple hours away. Even if he lived next door, I wouldn't have been allowed to see him. Jehovah's Witnesses don't date outsiders. But we exchanged room numbers anyway. The next morning, he called and asked to meet for breakfast. I said yes. I thought it would be the last time.

But a few days later, he called again. "What are you doing right now?" he asked. "I want to see you. I moved into my grandparents' house in your town for the summer."

He moved to see me. What was happening? Was this a dream? I didn't feel like I had a choice to make. The choice had already been made.

I started sneaking around. The lying was exhausting, but it let me see him. On our first date, we talked for hours. I asked him everything about his life, his family, his exes, his friends. I loved it all. We started seeing each other every day. He got a job where I was working, so it got easier.

But Mom got suspicious. One night, we were hanging wallpaper at a job site. I glanced out a second-story window and saw her getting out of her car.

"Hide!" I said. "Why?" Todd asked. "Just trust me." He ducked into a closet, confused. She came upstairs and started opening doors. I asked what she was doing. "Just looking," she said. Then she opened the closet.

"Hello," he said.
"I'm Beth. Who are you?"
"I'm Todd."

She turned and gave me that familiar look. Disgust and disdain. "Dena, come home. Now."

This time, I didn't shrink.

The panic was gone.

I looked her straight in the eyes and said, "No. I'll come home later."

Her face changed. She looked afraid.

The power had shifted.
And she knew it.

She tried to soften. "Come home. I'll put on a pot of coffee and we'll talk."

I didn't need to yell. I didn't need to win. I just said, "It's over, Mom. I'm done."

At home, she waited.

Her words, as always, found the lowest blow:

"You know it won't work.
He's too good looking for you."

It stung. A part of me still believed her words. But I'd already chosen to walk away.

I asked for a meeting with the elders and told them I wanted to be disfellowshipped. It felt strange and strong all at once. They tried to talk me out of it. "It's too bad," one said. "You were really good at bringing people into the truth."

Those were his words. Not "You matter." Not "Are you okay?" Just that I had been useful.

Dad and his new girlfriend were out of the country. They didn't want me around anyway.

So I loaded what little I had—some clothes, a stereo, a few records— and moved into my car. The construction trailer had a shower, and every evening I'd clean up and lock the door behind me. [A pen & ink drawing of your car & the construction trailer here.]

I was technically homeless. But I had never felt more free.

I was no longer surviving.

I was choosing.

Todd and I saw each other every day, falling harder with each one. I couldn't get enough of him. I wanted to know everything. His family. His friends. His story. But then it hit me.

He was going back to college in a month.

Panic set in.

What was I going to do?

Without giving it too much thought, I decided to keep moving forward.

"You go to college?" I asked one day.

He smiled. "Yeah."

"I think I want to go too."

I had $800 saved from hanging wallpaper. So I got in my car and drove four hours to Louisiana Tech. No tour. No idea what major to pick. I walked into the registrar's office, walked up to the counter, and said, "I'd like to sign up to go to school here."

The counselor looked at me like I'd just fallen off a turnip truck, but kindly. She asked about my high school classes. My ACT or SAT scores.

"I don't know what those are," I said honestly.

It was the 1980s. You could still enroll with some grit and a Pell Grant. She helped me apply for financial aid, arranged for me to start with non-credit courses, and explained I'd need to take the entrance exams soon.

I was elated.

I was going to college.

Todd and I soaked up every moment of that summer. When it came time to move in, everything I owned fit in my car. Clothes, a pillow, sheets, a blanket, my stereo. That was it.

My assigned roommates were best friends from high school. Their families were decorating their dorm sides with twinkle lights and matching bedspreads. They laughed and hugged and cried their goodbyes.

I made my bed in five minutes, shoved my crate under it, and sat down.

No tears. No send-off.

Just me and my crate.

But I was happy. For the first time, I'd chosen where to belong.

Classes were a mystery. I had no idea what I was doing. I chose fine art and interior design. Probably the most expensive major I could've picked. Supplies were outrageous. I bought used books when I could and borrowed everything else. I got a part-time job at a hardware store. Tried to study. Mostly, I majored in Todd Petty. (Ha.)

One professor eventually pulled me aside and said, "You should just marry someone rich and forget about all this."

It stung.

But I was used to that.

Honestly, I wasn't learning art or design as much as I was learning how to live. How to make friends. How to be a girlfriend. How to navigate someone else's family. Everything was new. Everything was foreign.

The first semester was hard. Todd and I weren't married; we were just dating. But to me, he was everything. My world. My anchor.

I was needy. I can see that now. I didn't know how to be in a healthy relationship, and he was still figuring out who he was too. We had the usual fights. Young love. Insecurity. Exhaustion.

But I didn't have anyone else.

I had a few friends, but not close ones. I had no family to lean on. So when Todd said he wanted to break up, it shattered me.

I was devastated.

I'd never had anyone before. No one I could trust. No one I belonged to. I realize now that I didn't even grieve leaving my parents. I didn't feel sad. I didn't feel torn. There was no bond to break. There was only silence and relief.

But Todd?

He was my first connection. My first safe place. My first taste of being seen and wanted. It wasn't just heartbreak. It was the collapse of the first place I'd ever felt like I belonged.

CHAPTER SEVEN:
WORKING THROUGH THE DARK SHADOWS

The Can of Tuna

In our dating, I had become reliant on us going back and forth, sharing money when needed. I'd give Todd part of my paycheck when he was low, and he'd do the same for me.

Just so happened, when we broke up, I was low. I had one can of tuna to last two days until my next paycheck. The panic hit hard. I wasn't eating much anyway. I was too sad. It was cold, rainy, and I was alone.

In a desperate moment, I called my mom.

"Oh, hey. What do you want?" she answered.

"I just wanted to say hi. See how everyone's doing."

A short, "We're fine."
Then silence.

"Well, I guess you don't want me to call anymore," I said.
She replied, "I think it would be best."

I hung up.

It was the lowest moment of my life.

The thought crossed my mind:
If I died, no one would mourn me.

I don't remember what the pills were or who they belonged to. I just remember swallowing as many as I could, lying down, hoping I'd fall asleep.

And not wake up.

A Miraculous Save

But God had different plans. I started vomiting and couldn't stop.

"Please," I prayed, "let me die."

My roommate called Todd. He picked me up and took me to the hospital.

I never told anyone what I'd done. They ran tests, said I had a bacterial infection, and sent me home. Todd gave me a place to rest and made sure I stayed hydrated.

I didn't tell a soul until just a few years ago; in a moment of raw honesty, I shared with the staff at Mentors Care.

A pastor I love once said, "Suicide is a permanent solution to a temporary problem." And it's true. But when you're in that moment, you can't see beyond it.

God saved me. And after that, He kept showing up. Little flickers of light. Small winks through people who didn't even realize they were being used.

Stranded and Seen

Todd and I got back together. We were dating again, and something in me had shifted. I was alive and I wanted to live.

One weekend, I left his parents' house to head back to school. It was nearly dark. Middle of nowhere. My old car sputtered and died on a two-lane highway.

No power steering. No help in sight.

I coasted to the shoulder. "Oh God, now what?" I muttered.

Until then, I hadn't really prayed. Not since leaving home. The god I'd known was angry. Cruel. The god of destruction and Armageddon. But that whisper of a prayer slipped out.

Moments later, a pickup truck pulled up behind me. A man with bright red hair approached. "Pop your hood."

As he tinkered under the hood, his wife and three red-haired kids got out. One of the littlest ran to me and said, "Swing me!"

And there we were, twirling in a ditch, laughing. A few minutes later, the man turned the key in my car and it started.

I offered him my last $20.
"Keep your money. Be safe."

And just like that, the red-haired family disappeared down the road.
Sometimes flashes of light only make the dark more obvious.

Chasing the Dream

I was back in school but still struggling. On academic probation.

Drowning.

The new women's golf team was forming, and Todd's friend asked me to play. "Yup, I play," I said, though I'd only really played when my dad let me tag along.

But I was hungry for life. I joined the golf team. I also walked onto the tennis team as a practice partner. Between school, work, and sports, I stayed busy.

One day, while hitting balls, an older man watched me.

"You have a natural swing," he said. "I want to coach you. For free."

He claimed to be one of the top 100 coaches in the world. And he really seemed to believe in me.

I started training with him: driving long distances, meeting his friends, hearing about his plans for my future. He said I had what it took to go pro.

But something about him felt off.

A Line I Wouldn't Cross

One day, he said, "You should pose nude. I know people. You could make a lot of money."

I felt sick. How did he know how desperate I was?

Just days earlier, I had told my dad I couldn't get to work without a new tire. He mailed me $20, his version of help. "You can get a good retread for that," he said.

It was the only money he ever sent.

That twenty-dollar bill made it clear: I was on my own.

And somehow, that man saw it too. He saw my need and wanted to use it.

But I said no.

It was a spiritual moment.

A crossroads.

I could've given in. I could've justified it. But something in me stood up.

"No," I said. "Not today. Not ever."

That day, something broke in the spirit. And something rose up in me. I didn't know what the future held, but I knew this: I had worth. I had a future.

And I wasn't for sale.

A Parable I Needed

I once heard a story:

A man lay drunk in the street. Rain began to fall. He woke up angry, stumbling along. A tiny kitten blocked his path.

He raised his foot to kick it but paused.

Looked in its eyes.

And stepped around it.

The angels watching asked Gabriel, "Can we give him one gift?"

Gabriel agreed.

With the gift, the man joined a support group.

Then came more gifts: he got sober, found a job, changed his life.

He grew rich in soul and spirit.

It all started with one small mercy.

I think about that story a lot.

Mercy multiplies.

So does faith.

And I was learning how to live in both.

Everyday Mentors and Heavenly Winks

My dreams came true when Todd and I finally started talking about getting married. He had graduated and found a job in Georgia. Once we set the date, I didn't waste any time planning. I'd never even been to a wedding outside the Jehovah's Witnesses. I had no idea what I was doing only that I was marrying the most wonderful man on the planet. I felt like the most blessed woman alive.

Dad's new wife offered to help with the planning. We decided on Todd's childhood Episcopal church. I bought fabric for my dress, and my Aunt Nell agreed to sew it. Dad said he'd pay for the food, so I thought we were set. But oh my gosh, so many details. So many expenses I hadn't even considered.

We met with the priest and chose the long version of the ceremony. When the big day arrived, I was ready. The groom's side of the church was full. My side? Maybe ten people. But I didn't care. I was happy.

I'd never been in another church before. Midway through the ceremony, it hit me. I was getting married in a place my mom would've called "the devil's house." The service included communion, and I had no idea what that even meant. I just knew it felt right.

Jehovah's Witnesses only observe communion once a year, at Passover. And only the 144,000 who claim to be "anointed" are allowed to partake. The rest just watch. In all my years, I'd only seen one person take communion.

But here I was, standing at the altar, shaking in my boots, taking the sacraments. I hadn't met the true God yet. I still believed He hated me. So I figured, what did it matter?

After we moved to a small town in Georgia, my journey of discovering who I really was, and who God really is, finally began.

God knew exactly what He was doing when He placed us next door to Mrs. Brown. She was a retired teacher and one of the kindest women I'd ever met. A couple of years into our marriage, Bryce was born. I had no clue what I was doing as a mom. But Mrs. Brown talked with me every week, gently offering her wisdom.

She read to children at the schools. Volunteered at her church. Helped others without expecting anything in return. She was the kind of woman who gave back just because it was in her nature.

One day, she overheard me losing my temper with Bryce. Later, she gently said, "Being a mother can drain us. When we're exhausted, we say and do things we regret. All mothers wish we could do it better. So make time to rest. Get a babysitter. You and Todd need time together."

No guilt.
No condemnation.
Just care and compassion.

Not long after, I met some older women from church who played golf once a week and invited me to join. I didn't go every week, but when I did, we laughed. A lot. They offered marital advice (not always the best advice, I'd later learn), but their hearts were in the right place, and I appreciated their warmth.

Like in college, I was noticed for how far I could drive the ball. A golf pro offered to coach me for free. After talking it over with Todd, we decided I should give it a try.

Before long, I was introduced to a man who offered to sponsor me. That meant I could quit my part-time job and focus on golf full-time. I applied for professional status with the LPGA (Ladies Professional Golf Association) and signed away my amateur eligibility. Looking back, I question: What was I thinking? Just like when I enrolled in college, I wasn't prepared at all.

I entered my first professional women's tournament on the Futures Tour. The first few were close to home, but I wasn't good enough to make the cut. I came home after just a few days. Todd was supportive. After a few more tries, I realized I wasn't where I was supposed to be. I was chasing something but didn't know what. I missed home. I missed Todd and Bryce. I wasn't sure what I was meant to be doing.

Working Through the Dark Shadows

During one of those tournaments, after a particularly bad round, I stood on the 18th green in tears. I couldn't stop crying. For the first time, I prayed a real prayer:

God, where are You?
What am I supposed to do?
Do You hate me?

It wasn't about golf. It was about the ache inside me. I had a beautiful life, but I still felt lost.

Even so, God was guiding me. Nudging me. Giving me little winks from heaven to let me know He was there. I found this entry in my golf journal—proof that even golf had become His classroom:

"If you can hit out of a bunker, you can get yourself through anything. The lip is above your head. You hit blind over a berm. You look at your ball. You imagine where it should land. You ground yourself. You choke down. You don't flinch. You swing hard. Big. Fearless. The sand flies. You're blind for a moment. But when you reach the top—you just might find the ball three inches from the hole."

It seemed like every turn in life was a bunker shot.

Eventually, Todd's new job brought us to Birmingham, Alabama. We didn't know anyone, but we packed up and took another leap of faith. That's where Lexie was born. Bryce started playing T-ball. Life kept moving.

And that's where I met Ms. Sue and Ms. Francis.

They were two older women who had made a pact to care for each other after their husbands died. I met them at the ball field. Ms. Sue was watching her grandson. She was an artist and insisted I get back to painting. She even gave me a box of supplies: "Get your canvas, paint, and linseed oil out. Get to work."

She was right. It felt good to paint again.

They both fell in love with baby Lexie. And I fell in love with them.

Ms. Sue had raised five children alone after her husband died of cancer. She painted portraits to support her family. She was one of the strongest women I've ever met.

Ms. Francis was a devout Catholic and best friends with Mother Angelica, the nun from the cable TV show. She taught theology to nuns and was deeply respected in her church. A Cardinal had even honored her, and she proudly displayed the medal in her kitchen. She once told me, beaming, that her ecclesiastical rank was even higher than the Kennedys.

She wasn't boastful.
Just proud of her walk with Jesus.

I asked her a million questions about God, and she answered every one with patience and grace. She mentored me about life, marriage, parenting, my past, and most of all, my walk with Christ. Even as her body declined, her mind stayed sharp. Her faith never wavered.

Once, I said to her, "I'm so sorry you're hurting."
She smiled and said, "I'm just suffering with my Jesus."

Those words pierced my soul.
We all suffer.
But how we suffer tells a story.

Do we scream, "Why me?" and accuse God of abandoning us? Or do we lean in, even through the pain, and whisper, "You suffered first for me. Now I'll suffer with You by my side."

In honor of Ms. Francis, I painted her portrait and called it *Into the Light*.

I tried to capture her frailty, the steps that must have hurt so deeply and also her joy. Her hope. Her quiet anticipation of being with Jesus.

She was dearly loved. And is dearly missed.

CHAPTER EIGHT:
THE POWER OF JOY & HEALING

Living Testimony

Todd took another job—this time in Cabot, Arkansas. And I loved it. We were closer to Aunt Nell and Uncle Tommy, and we quickly found a little church we liked.

After visiting a few times, I asked if a pastor could stop by the house so I could ask some questions. He came by, kind and patient, taking his time to talk with us.

A Nudge from God

Then something unexpected happened.

"We're having a revival this weekend," he said. "Would you share your testimony?"

I blinked. "Why me?"

He smiled. "I don't know. I just think you're supposed to."

He knew nothing about my past. We hadn't even gone that deep in conversation. But I said yes.

When the night came, Todd stayed home with the kids. Looking back, I believe that was part of God's plan.

I stood there and began to tell my story. The tears came, and I noticed they weren't mine alone. People in the congregation were crying too. At one point, I couldn't go on. I was completely overwhelmed.

I looked over at the senior pastor, Richard. He wiped a tear from his own cheek and gave me a gentle smile. In that moment, he felt like a kind uncle, giving me courage just with his eyes. I kept going.

"I realized God knew me," I said. "He loved me even before I knew Him."

That moment was divine. It had been planned long before I ever drew breath. The pastor hugged me, and I sat down. Spent, but at peace.

A woman stepped up to the piano and began playing a song I had never heard before: *He touched me, oh, He touched me—and oh, the joy that floods my soul...*[7]

Something happened. I felt it. I knew it. I had been touched by the living God.

I sat in awe, flooded with emotion. It was as if the words were written just for me. Shackled by shame, guilt, and fear, now suddenly overwhelmed by peace.

That moment marked a turning point in my story.

Something shifted in the Spirit, and I would never be the same.

It was as if God whispered, *It's time. Come. Follow Me. Let Me lead you—you're ready.*

For the first time, I began to truly understand who Jesus was. He wasn't just the Son of God, not just a figure I'd heard about growing up. He was God. And He wanted me to know Him. Personally. Deeply.

I was hungry to learn. I started reading the Bible, praying more deeply, and volunteering with the youth. I couldn't get enough.

About a year later, the church called me in for a meeting.

"We'd like to offer you the position of youth pastor," they said. "Interim?" I asked. Surely they didn't mean *the* youth pastor. I'd never even been to a youth group. I was still new to the faith. No training. I'd only helped out at a few events.

"Yes," the pastor said. "We think you're it."

I told them I needed to pray and talk to Todd. At the time, the youth group had about ten kids. It was struggling and needed healing. Bryce was seven. Lexie was two. I said I'd take it on part-time if I could get some training.

The church agreed and sent me to a Youth Specialties conference in California. I came back with a notebook full of ideas, a heart full of prayer, and a quiet fire in my spirit.

The Second Time

The group grew quickly. I rallied volunteers, built momentum, and dove in. The "part-time" idea disappeared fast. Balancing it all with family wasn't easy but it was worth it.

Eventually, I started asking deeper questions: Were the kids just having fun, or were they growing? Were we making disciples?

So I created *The 12-Step Discipleship Walk*—a guide based on what Jesus modeled. Twelve steps to help teens live a life that followed Christ.

The students responded. They grew. The group grew. It was amazing. And exhausting.

Then came the mission trip.

We chose an inner-city church in Memphis that fed over 100 homeless people a day. Our job was to clean, sort, paint, and serve wherever needed. It was eye-opening: drug houses, deep poverty, and despair. And still, the kids served with joy.

One day, the pastor pulled me aside.

"Tell me about you," he said.

So I did.

Then he asked, "You're coming to church Sunday before you leave, right?"

"Yes," I said. "We're all looking forward to it."

"Would you share your testimony?"

I hesitated. "No offense, but I don't think these folks want to hear about me. They've suffered so much more than I ever have."

"If the Spirit leads you, will you?"

"Of course."

He Touched Me Again

That Sunday, the church was full. Mostly people from the street. The worship was powerful, raw, and real. Then the pastor stood and said, "Now, Dena Petty is going to give her testimony."

Guess the Spirit led him already, I thought, half-laughing.

I stood up and told my story again, tears flowing. But again, they weren't mine alone. After I finished and sat down, the worship leader stepped up to the mic. And just like before, she began to sing *He Touched Me*.

I was stunned.

After the service, I went to her. "You're not going to believe this," I said. "That same song was sung the first time I ever gave my testimony."

She blinked. "You're not going to believe this, I forgot the song I was supposed to sing. I went blank. I just started singing whatever came to mind."

The pianist chimed in. "Yeah, I had no idea what was happening. I just followed her lead."

Another wink from God.

Another reminder: *I see you. I love you. You're mine.*

You have a future.
You have a purpose.
You are made whole.

SECTION THREE:

Sparking a Flame

CHAPTER NINE:
LOOKING BACK; MOVING FORWARD

Connecting the Dots

I believe in generational trauma. When left unhealed, it becomes a curse passed from one generation to the next like an invisible weight. Pain, shame, and dysfunction go unchecked and unspoken. My parents carried those burdens deep in their bones. Their hurt became their identity.

Every moment of my life, too many to recount in one book, shaped me into who I am today. Eventually, we moved to Midlothian, Texas, and something shifted. I grew into someone confident and bold. I became a woman healed and whole. But even as I felt ready for something new, God said, *Wait*. It was a season to fully embrace being a wife and mother. One of rest, even though I stayed busy.

Lexie settled in quickly. I volunteered at school events, helped with her activities, and cheered her on in volleyball. Bryce stood out as a quarterback and was already being scouted for college. Todd was launching a new architectural precast plant, and we were all thriving in our own lanes. The foundation had been laid, and God was at the center of it all. And for the first time, I believed the generational trauma stopped with me.

God had shown up at every turn. Sometimes, I only recognized His fingerprints in hindsight. But He had always been there.

A New Assignment

After Bryce committed to Baylor University, the whirlwind of recruiting settled. That's when our high school principal approached me with a request:

"Would you start a mentoring program?"

I knew deep down in my soul that this was it. This was what all the struggle had prepared me for. While Lexie was in school, I could invest in the lives of students like me: the overlooked, the at-risk, the ones hanging on by a thread.

I said yes.

And so, Mentors Care was born.

I drafted a plan, wrote curriculum, and studied what worked in other nonprofits. I found a broom-closet-turned-book-drop in the school library and asked if I could use it as an office. It was perfect. I added a desk, some chairs, a computer, and a phone. Then I got to work.

At first, the principal hoped we'd find 10 to 15 mentors. We ended up with 30, each paired with a student. I reminded the mentors of their meetings. I held the students accountable with updated grades and attendance. This mattered. This was ministry. Meeting people where they were and showing them, they mattered.

I thought of the students I served as mirrors of myself. Lonely. Forgotten. In need of someone who cared.

Collateral Hope

Out of my own life came *Talking Points*: lessons I wrote for the program based on hard-earned truths. Many of these students weren't being taught the basics at home. Some were in crisis. Others were simply lost. They needed tools. Encouragement. Grace. I knew, because I had been one of them.

As Albert Einstein is often quoted as saying, "Nothing happens until something moves."[8]

The Whisper, the Wink

When I reflect on all the darkness—hopelessness, guilt, rejection—I see how fiercely God fought to keep my light from going out. He whispered truth. He winked in moments I might have otherwise missed. Each whisper reminded me: *You were made to live, love, thrive, create, and flourish.*

Sometimes I only understood in hindsight. The night I tried to end my life, or the day my car broke down and a family of redheads showed up to help me. Looking back, those weren't coincidences. They were divine interventions. God was saying, *I see you. I love you. You're not alone.*

And then there were the crossroads, the moments when I had to choose. I walked away from a toxic mother, a guilt-heavy religion, a father who didn't protect me, and a path paved with easy money that would've left me empty. Those choices weren't easy. But they were necessary.

I hit rock bottom more than once. But instead of accumulating damage, I gathered resilience. I call it collateral hope: the redemptive possibility that emerges when belief wins over bitterness.

Redemption Is Real

I've often heard people say, "There's no way that's your story. You don't seem like someone who's lived through all that." And I smile. Not out of pride, but gratitude. I say, "Thank You, Jesus." He redeemed me. Delivered me. Made me new.

But redemption wasn't magic. I had to do the work. I had to ask hard questions:

> "Why did I think that?"
> "Why did I say that?"
> "Why did I react that way?"

Healing demanded honesty. Self-examination. Emotional and spiritual renovation.

The Power of Belief

In an article titled *The Power of Belief,* Focus3 writes:

> "Belief creates resilience… Belief doesn't just survive adversity; it gets stronger because of it… It sustains your vision and strengthens your will. It makes you stronger because of the adversity you are forced to endure."[9]

That's what belief has done in me. It made me stronger. Not just the strength that comes from belief in myself, but belief that God saw me, loved me, and was with me.

The Mud Puddle

I've told my students that we sometimes live our lives in a mud puddle. It's familiar even if it's miserable. A mentor might reach out a hand and say, *Come out of that. There's something better.* And if we're brave, we might take their hand and step out… only to look around and say, *This feels uncomfortable. I don't belong here.*

And sometimes we jump right back in.

But healing means staying out of the puddle. Choosing something unfamiliar for the sake of growth. And when we feel stuck, God has a way of moving us forward.

The Vision

I remember crying out to God, asking Him to stop the replay of pain in my mind. And He gave me a vision.

I saw myself sitting beside a river under a majestic tree. It was peaceful. Bright. Then behind me, a wall rose from the ground like a mausoleum stacked with drawers. I knew what to do. I opened a drawer and began pulling dark, sticky film-like memories from my mind, and placing them inside. One by one, I buried the pain. The replay stopped. The heaviness lifted.

My pastor later said, "That was a mausoleum. God let you bury it."

And I believe that's exactly what happened. God didn't want me to carry the weight anymore. Redemption means release. Once forgiven, we are free.

Legacy and Light

Through Christ, there is hope, healing, and a new path forward. One that's not just for me, but for my children and their children. The generational trauma that haunted me has been broken.

I still think about that time as a little girl, standing in shark-infested waters while my dad told me to cast a net. It's a picture of how unsafe my childhood felt.

But God...

God protected me when my earthly father did not. God has always been near.

I See You. I Hear You.

One of the greatest gifts we can offer another person is presence. Not fixing. Not preaching. Just showing up with open hands and a listening heart.

I've learned that my story isn't just mine, it's meant to be shared. As followers of Jesus, we don't keep our stories hidden. We tell them so others can see the hope we've found.

Working with teens for over 25 years, I've come to believe this: one caring adult really can change a life. You may be stepping into a relationship with someone whose past is shaped by 4,094 ancestors over 12 generations. You're not just mentoring a student. You're disrupting a cycle. Introducing hope.

That's what it means to be a mentor. To be the whisper. To be the wink.

THE PRACTICE OF O.N.E.

It starts with YOU:

>Open spiritual eyes

Pray to know who you really are. Forgive yourself. See yourself the way God sees you.

>Notice the needs of others

Practice empathy. We're all connected. Let compassion move you.

>Engage with intention

Be present. Advocate with love. Be the vessel God uses to give someone hope.

CLOSING PRAYER

Heavenly Father,

Thank You for healing and hope.

Help us live lives that glorify You
not by chasing our own desires,
but by following Yours.

May we live authentically, fully,
and freely in Jesus' name.

Amen.

ACKNOWLEDGMENTS

Writing a book is hard. For me, I was always told, "You have to tell your story!" But where to begin? None of this would be possible without my newfound friends, and some longtime friends, who guided and directed me along the way.

First, I want to thank Lannette Pottle of She Gets Published at www.shegetspublished.com for your professional guidance coaching me through the maze of starting, organizing, and holding me accountable. The start of my book was in the perfect setting with the perfect person.

To my editor, Cher Stein of The Write Perspective, thank you for your steady guidance, editorial wisdom, and genuine care for this story. Your insight, patience, and belief in this book made a lasting difference, and I'm deeply grateful for the way you walked with me through this process. I truly felt your sincere interest and passion for this project.

To my longtime friends, family, mentors, and the many along the way who encouraged me and inspired me to live life to the fullest, which includes writing this book … thank you!

I especially thank my Lord and Savior, Jesus Christ, for loving me even before I knew you. Thank you for redeeming my story and giving me the courage to tell it. I pray I have been a good steward of this new redeemed life you have given me.

ABOUT THE AUTHOR

Dena Petty is a speaker, author, and mentor committed to helping others discover purpose, strength, and hope—especially in the midst of difficult seasons.

In 2009, she founded **Mentors Care**, a 501(c)(3) nonprofit organization created to provide at-risk high school students with the guidance and support they need to graduate and reach their full potential. Built from the ground up, Mentors Care reflects Dena's deep belief in the power of presence, consistency, and personal investment. She developed a four-year curriculum for the program and co-authored a mentor guide to equip volunteers for meaningful, lasting impact.

Collateral Hope, a nonfiction work that shares her personal journey through darkness into faith, healing, and purpose. The story behind the book mirrors the heart of Mentors Care—finding hope in the mess and discovering that even the most painful chapters can lead to restoration and calling.

Through her speaking, mentoring, and writing, Dena empowers both students and volunteers to recognize their value and walk confidently into their own stories of growth and redemption. Today, Mentors Care serves more than 850 students with the support of 800 mentors across 20 high schools, and Dena remains committed to expanding the program's reach—changing lives one student, one mentor, and one story at a time.

MENTORS CARE

Mentorship for Meaningful Lives

Our Mission: Connecting struggling high school students with mentors, tools, and resources to help lead them towards graduation and purposeful lives.

We Match Students With Mentors

Over the course of 8 months, mentors spend approximately 1 hour each week with their respective students reviewing grades, going over assignments, and assessing strengths and areas for improvement. Our mentors are specially trained and equipped with our proven 24 Talking Points© system and other program materials designed to help students develop healthy self-perception and awareness of the many opportunities that abound in the world around them.

We're looking to make a difference.

Mentors Care.

ENDNOTES

1 Cherokee Heritage Center. "Trail of Tears Roll (1835–1838)."

2 The Dawes Act of 1887 was a U.S. federal law intended to assimilate Native Americans by dividing communal tribal land into individual allotments. Eligible individuals received parcels—typically 160 acres for heads of household—as recorded in the Dawes Rolls between 1898 and 1914. These allotments were meant to support self-sufficient farming but often led to significant land loss through forced sales, taxation, or fraud. See U.S. National Archives, "The Dawes Act," https://www.archives.gov/milestone-documents/dawes-act; and Claudio Saunt, *Unworthy Republic: The Dispossession of Native Americans and the Road to Indian Territory* (W. W. Norton & Company, 2020).

3 L. A. Kellstedt & C. E. Smidt, "Measuring Fundamentalism …" in *Religion and the Culture Wars* (1991).

4 *The Watchtower*, May 2011, Watch Tower Bible and Tract Society of Pennsylvania.

5 Watch Tower Bible and Tract Society of Pennsylvania, *Keep Yourselves in God's Love* (1980), referring to quote.

6 National Library of Medicine, "What Happens to Those Who Exit Jehovah's Witnesses: An Investigation of the Impact of Shunning," December 31, 2022, https://www.ncbi.nlm.nih.gov/pmc/articles/PMC9803876/.

7 "He Touched Me," lyrics by William J. Gaither. Used in brief for illustrative purposes only.

8 Commonly attributed to Albert Einstein; source unverified.

9 Focus3. *The Power of Belief*. Accessed July 30, 2025. https://focus3.com/the-power-of-belief/.

9 798993 485300